Boston

Contents

Visit Boston......................4

Freedom Trail.....................6

Art...............................12

Sport.............................13

A Trip up the Coast...........14

SCHOLASTIC

Published in the UK by
Scholastic Education, 2024
Scholastic Distribution Centre, Bosworth Avenue,
Tournament Fields, Warwick, CV34 6UQ
Scholastic Ireland, 89E Lagan Road, Dublin
Industrial Estate, Glasnevin, Dublin, D11 HP5F

Printed by Ashford Colour Press

This book is made of materials from
well-managed, FSC®-certified forests
and other controlled sources.

A CIP catalogue record for this book is available
from the British Library.

ISBN 978-0702-32724-7

Author
Rachel Russ

Editorial team
Rachel Morgan, Vicki Yates, Jane Jackson,
Jennie Clifford

Design team
Dipa Mistry, Andrea Lewis and We Are Grace

Photographs
Cover Mihai_Andritoiu/Shutterstock
p4–5, 16 DenisTangneyJr/iStock
p1, 4, 16 (American flag) Viktorija Reuta/
Shutterstock
p6 (main) gangliu10/iStock
p6 (inset), 16 dosecreative/iStock
p7 (park) Travellaggio/Shutterstock
p7 (boats) Justin Smith/iStock
p8 lunamarina/Shutterstock
p9 (background) Ink Drop/Shutterstock
p9 (top) Joseph Sohm/Shutterstock
p9 (middle) Sean Pavone/Shutterstock
p9 (bottom) CO Leong/Shutterstock
p10 (main) Pgiam/iStock
p10 (inset) mphillips007/iStock
p11 CHUYN/iStock
p12 (main), 16 Yegor Pavlovskyi/Shutterstock
p12 (inset) BearFotos/Shutterstock
p13 (top) FatCamera/iStock
p13 (bottom), 16 peepo/iStock
p13 (baseball) Willard/iStock
p14–15, 16 Chris Roe/Shutterstock

How to use this book

This book practises words with more than one consonant next to each other, plus long vowel sounds (like '**tr**ail' or '**str**eet'). Here are some examples from the book:

sport   freedom   trail   streets   coast

This book uses these common tricky words:

to   you   some   the   there   are   all
of   do   go   like   here   out   be

Before reading

- Read the title and look at the cover. Discuss what the book might be about.

During reading

- If necessary, sound out and then blend the sounds to read the word: p-ai-n-t-i-ng-s, paintings.
- Pause every so often to talk about the information.

After reading

- Talk about what has been read. Look at page 16 and discuss the images shown.

Visit Boston

Boston has lots to offer, from historic sights to thrilling sport.

You can visit its landmarks, see some paintings or chill in the park.

There are all sorts of things to do.

Freedom Trail

See sights for free along the Freedom Trail.

Look for the red-brick trail in the streets.

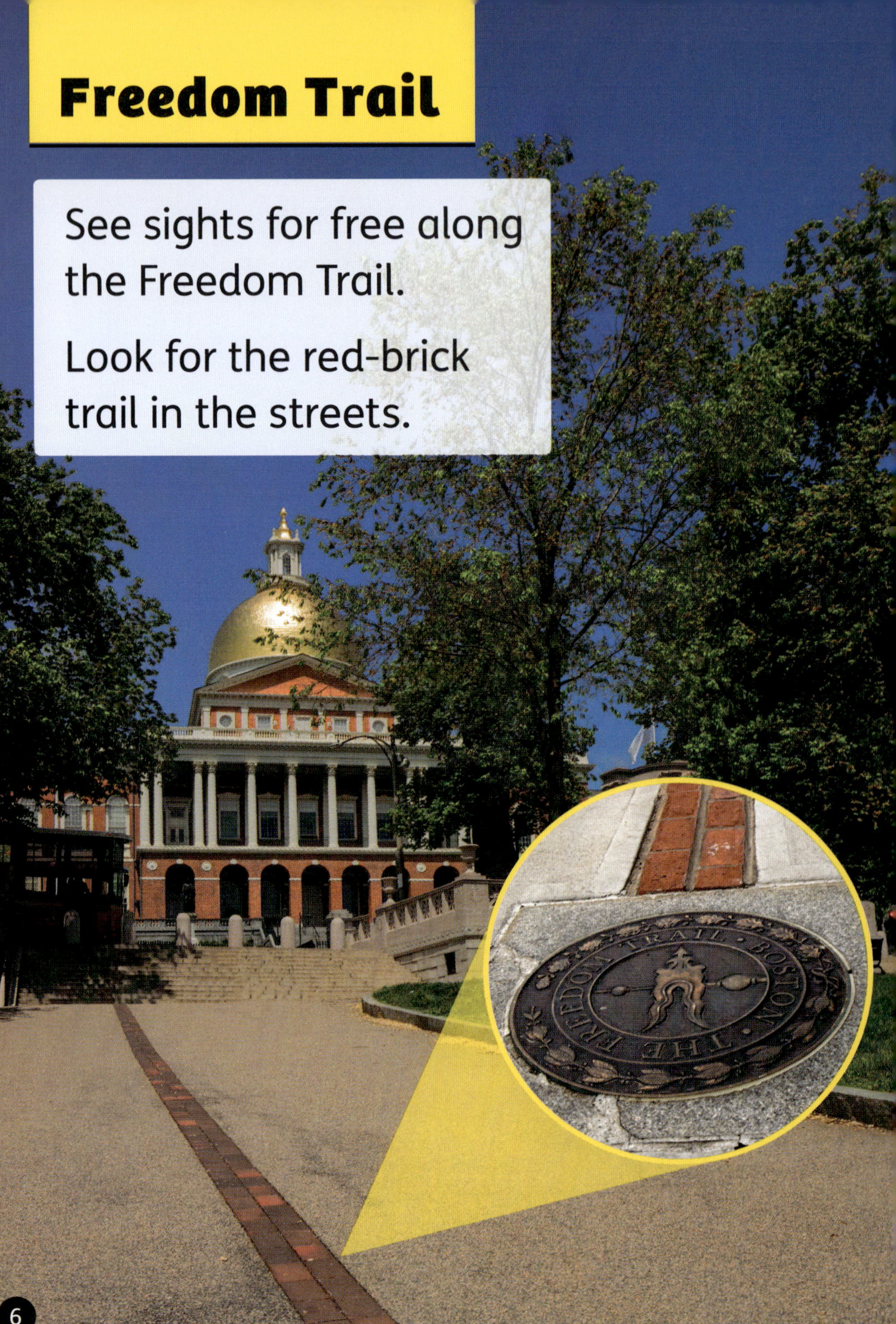

The trail starts at Boston Common.

Sit under the trees there or go on
the boats.

Park Street Church is near the common.
It is a Boston landmark.

Travel the streets of Boston and see some stunning sights.

Grab some lunch at Boston's historic market.

lobster sub

Bunker Hill is the point the Freedom Trail ends. But there is still lots to do!

If you like art, stop here to check out the bright paintings.

Sport

Sports fans can go and see the Boston Red Sox. There is a big crowd.

A Trip up the Coast

From Boston, go on a boat trip up the unspoiled coast. You might spot a humpback.

If you go sightseeing in Boston, you will not be disappointed!

Boston

Visit Boston p4

Freedom Trail p6

Art p12

Sport p13

A Trip up the Coast p14